General Care of Horses

worming a horse

dressing a wound

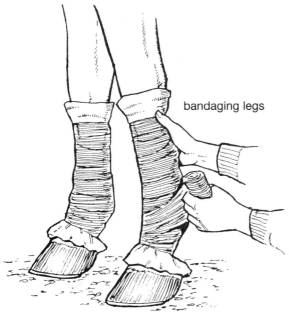

bandaging legs

checking pulse

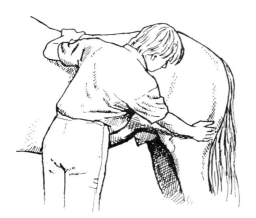

checking horse all over for signs of
inflammation: heat, swelling, and pain

examining the mouth

General Care of Horses

using clippers

trimming ears

trimming heels

trimming face

trimming tail

General Care of Horses

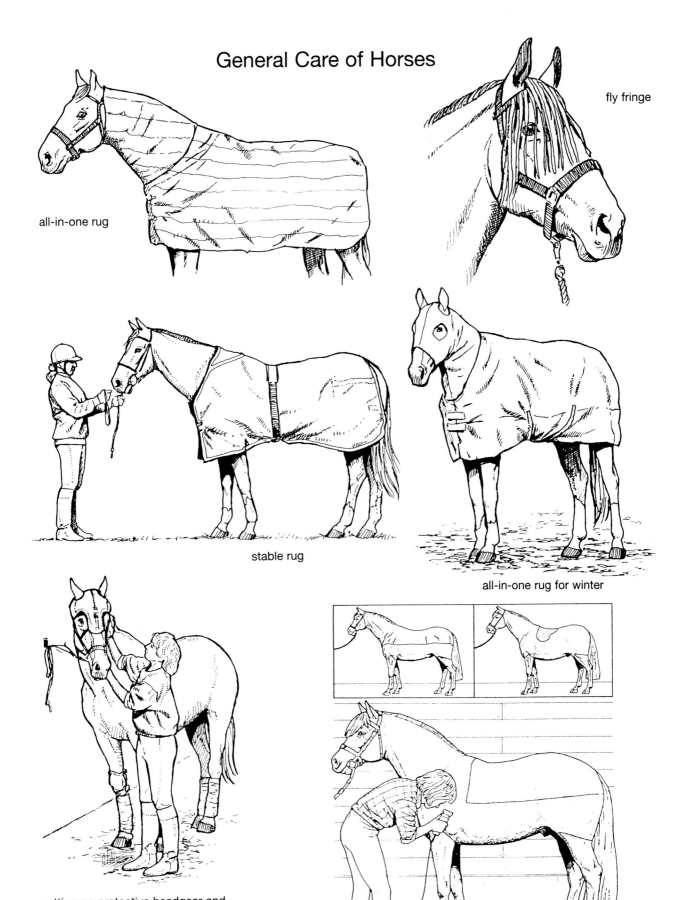

all-in-one rug

fly fringe

stable rug

all-in-one rug for winter

putting on protective headgear and
leg and knee boots

Types of Clip
trace clip, saddle or hunter clip, and blanket clip

3

Horse's Feet

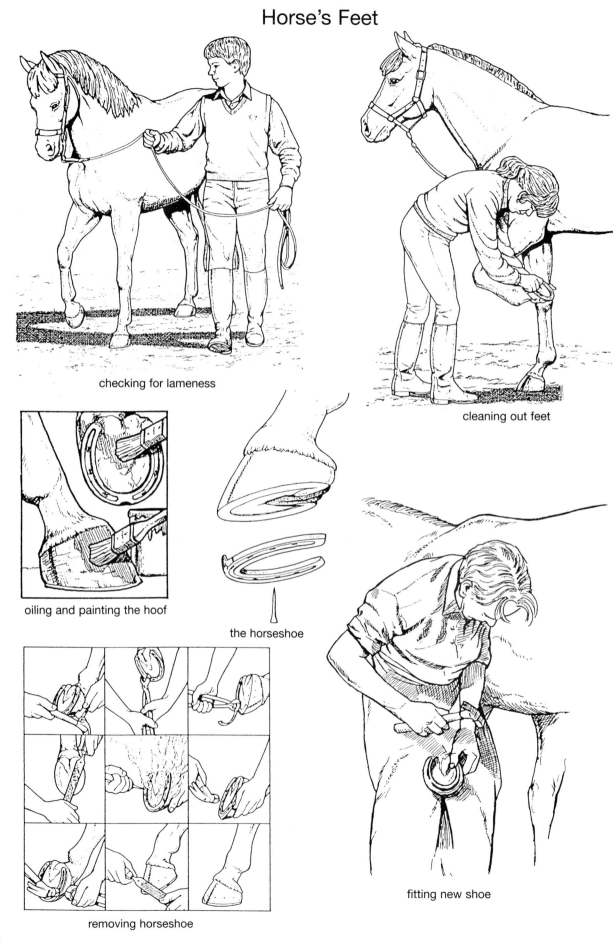

checking for lameness

cleaning out feet

oiling and painting the hoof

the horseshoe

removing horseshoe

fitting new shoe

Grooming a Horse

cleaning mane

washing tail

cleaning muzzle with soft sponge

grooming horse by quartering

using a stable rubber

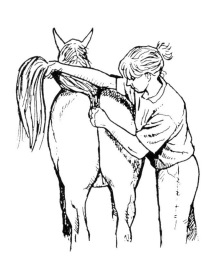

cleaning the dock

Grooming Horse—Preparing for a Show

using body brush and currycomb

combing mane

polishing coat

cleaning tail

wisping

cleaning head and eyes

Grooming Horse—Preparing for a Show

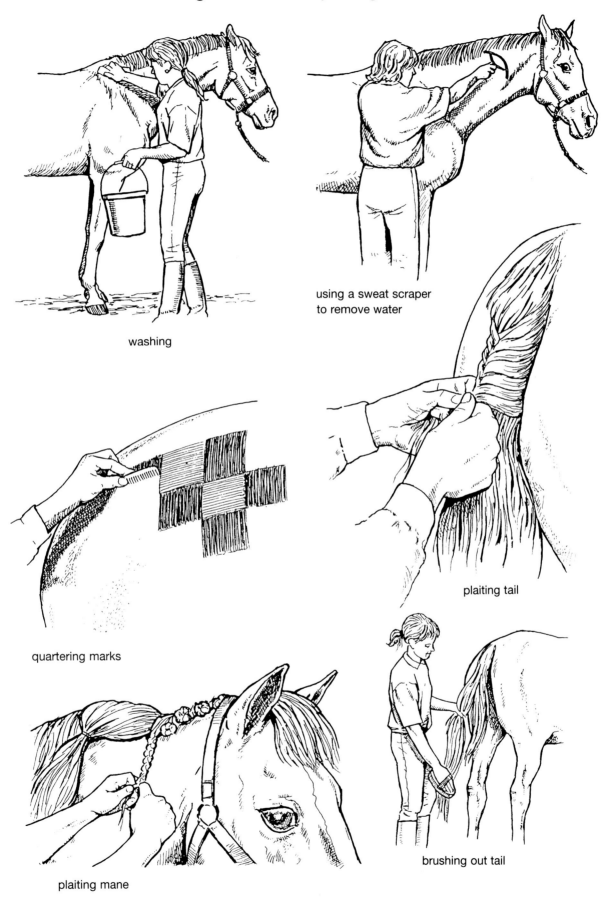

washing

using a sweat scraper to remove water

quartering marks

plaiting tail

plaiting mane

brushing out tail

Feeding

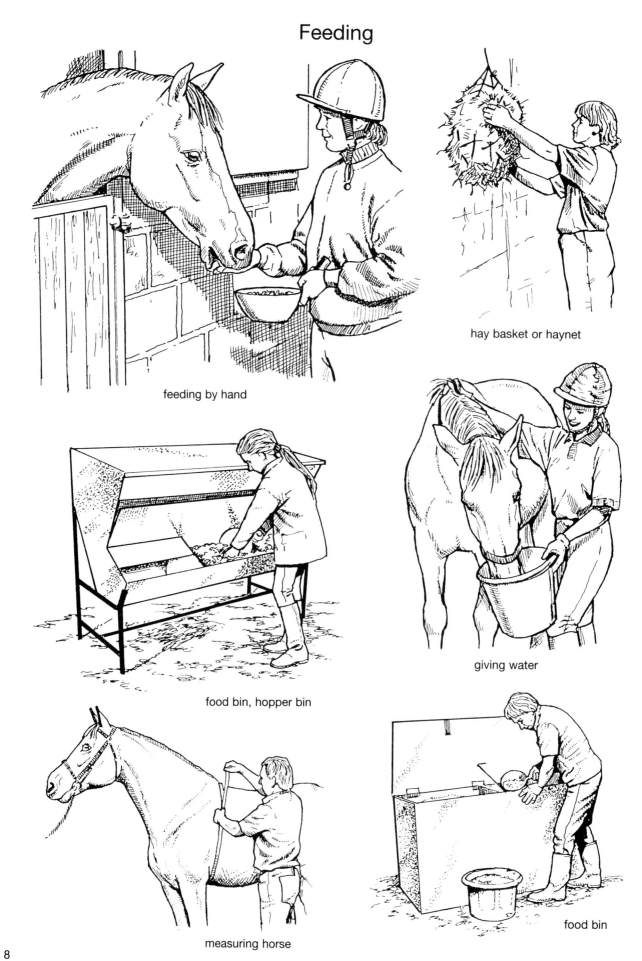

feeding by hand

hay basket or haynet

food bin, hopper bin

giving water

measuring horse

food bin

General Care, Mucking Out the Stable

mucking out with horse in stable

mucking out dirty bedding

brushing stable floor

separating clean straw

mucking out wood shavings

forking in clean shavings

Handling a Horse

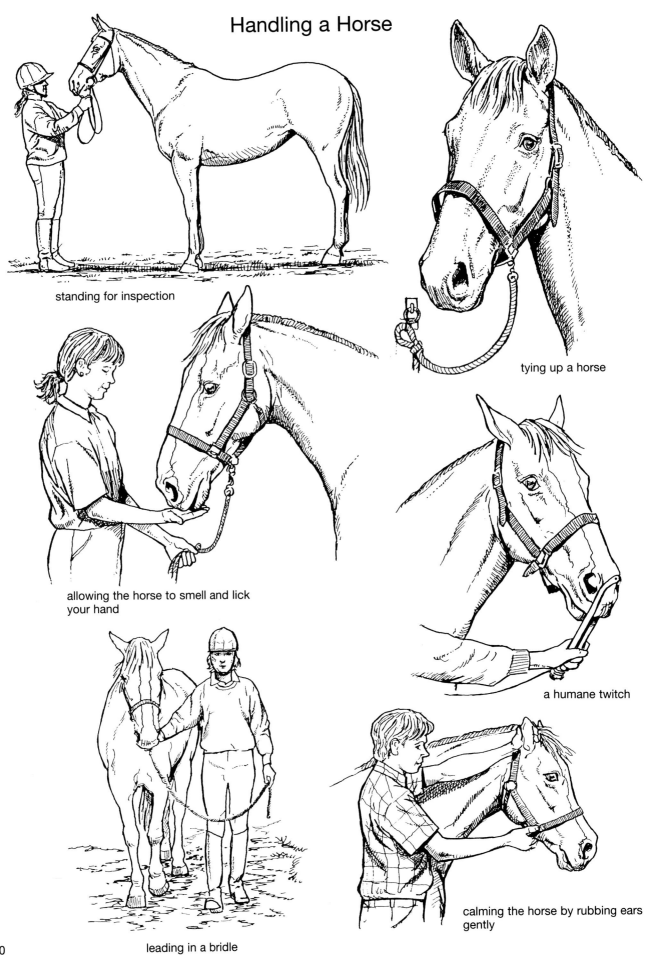

standing for inspection

tying up a horse

allowing the horse to smell and lick your hand

a humane twitch

leading in a bridle

calming the horse by rubbing ears gently

10

Handling a Horse

approaching horse in field

head collar

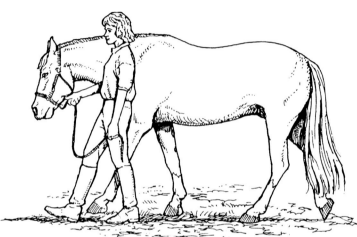

leading in a head collar

turning around

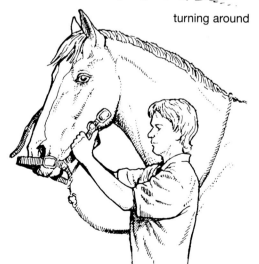

rope halter

fitting head collar

The Stable

Horse Trailers

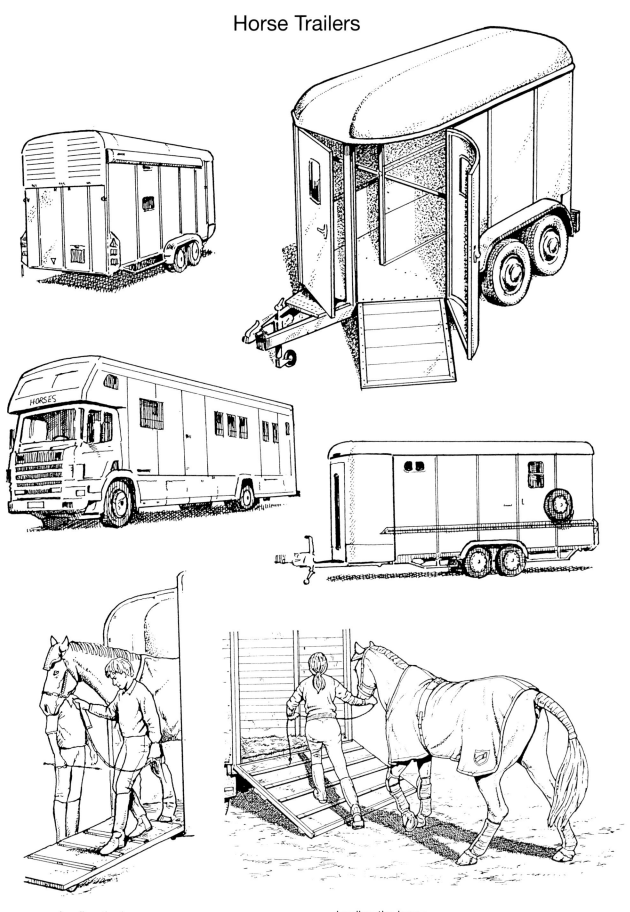

unloading the horse   loading the horse

Clothing

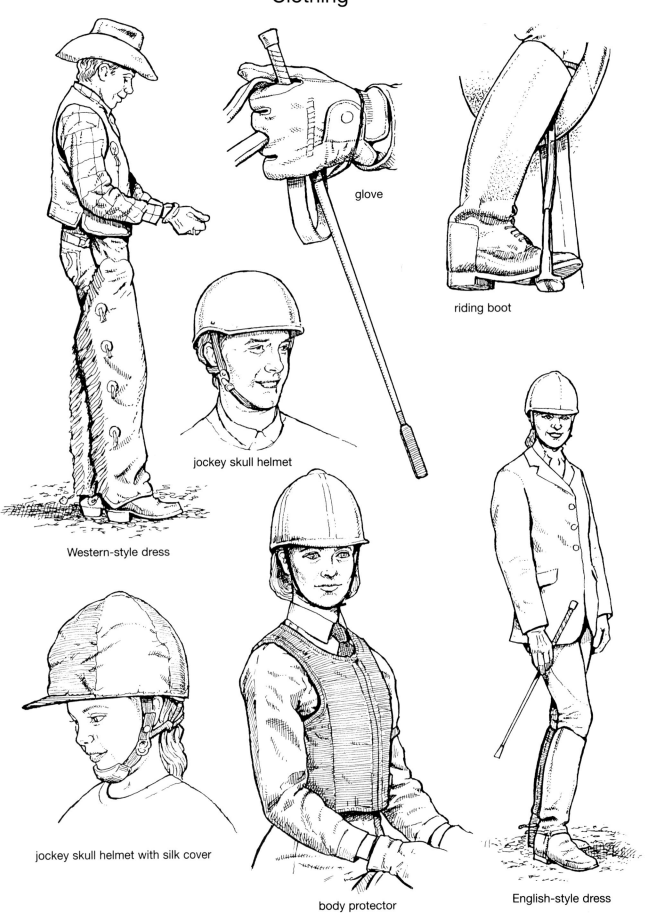

glove

riding boot

jockey skull helmet

Western-style dress

jockey skull helmet with silk cover

body protector

English-style dress

Exercises for the Rider

In the Saddle

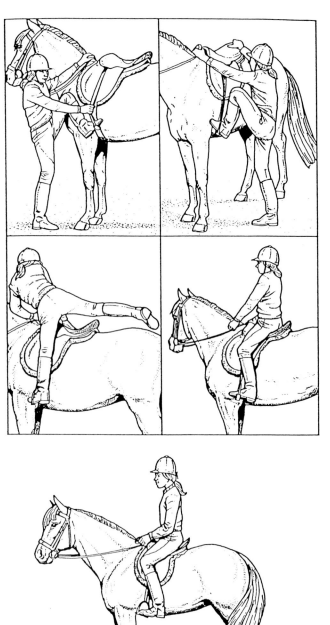

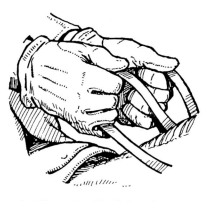

holding reins, English style

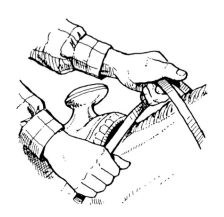

Western style

mounting and dismounting the horse

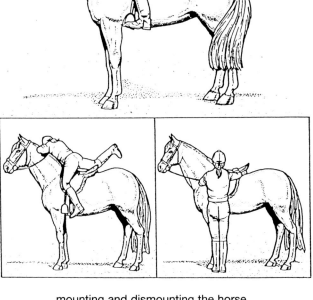

turning right

In the Saddle

trot

gallop

correct seat

halt

correct seat

17

Schooling Aids

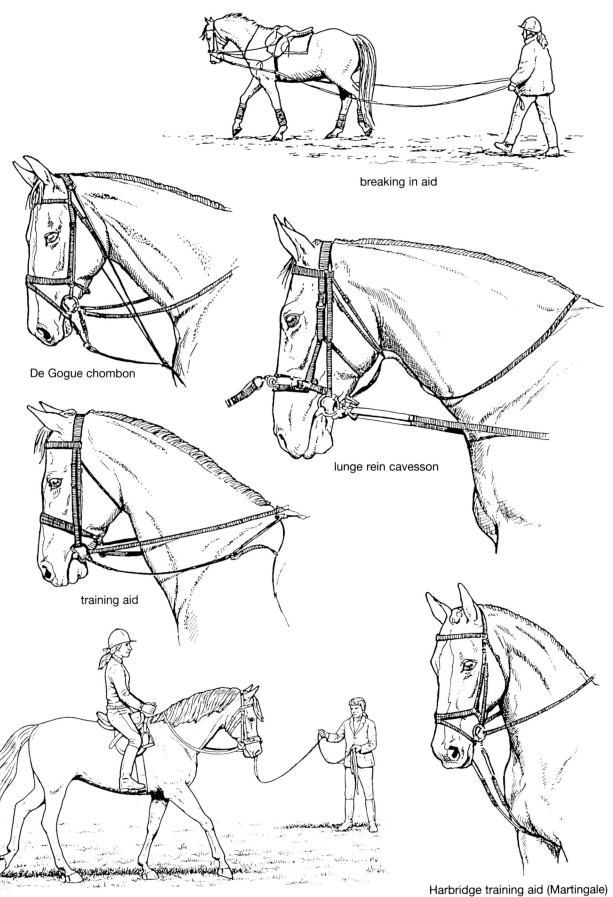

breaking in aid

De Gogue chombon

lunge rein cavesson

training aid

lunge rein in use

Harbridge training aid (Martingale)

Learning to Jump

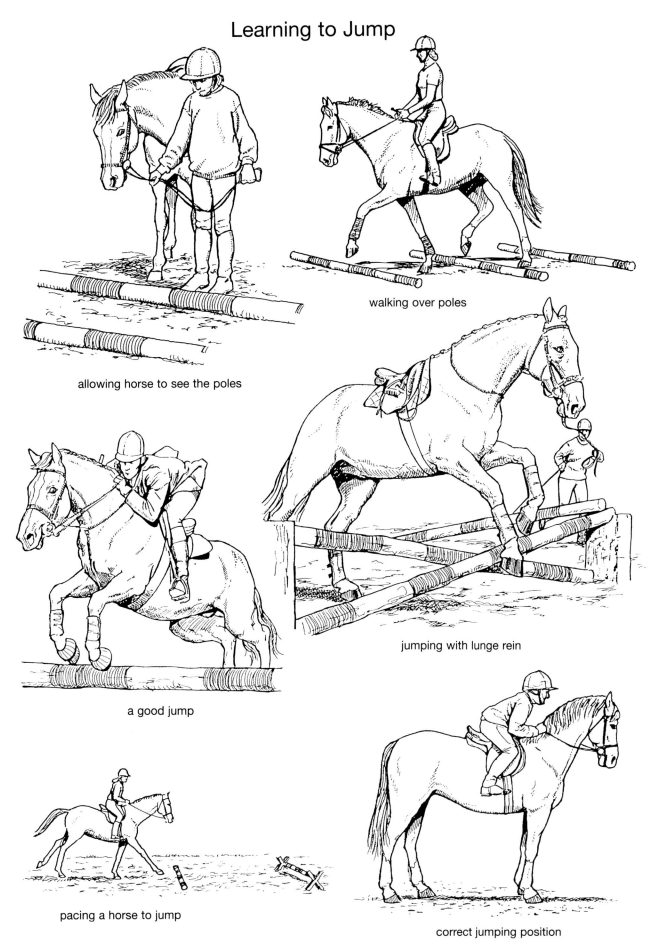

walking over poles

allowing horse to see the poles

jumping with lunge rein

a good jump

pacing a horse to jump

correct jumping position

Saddles

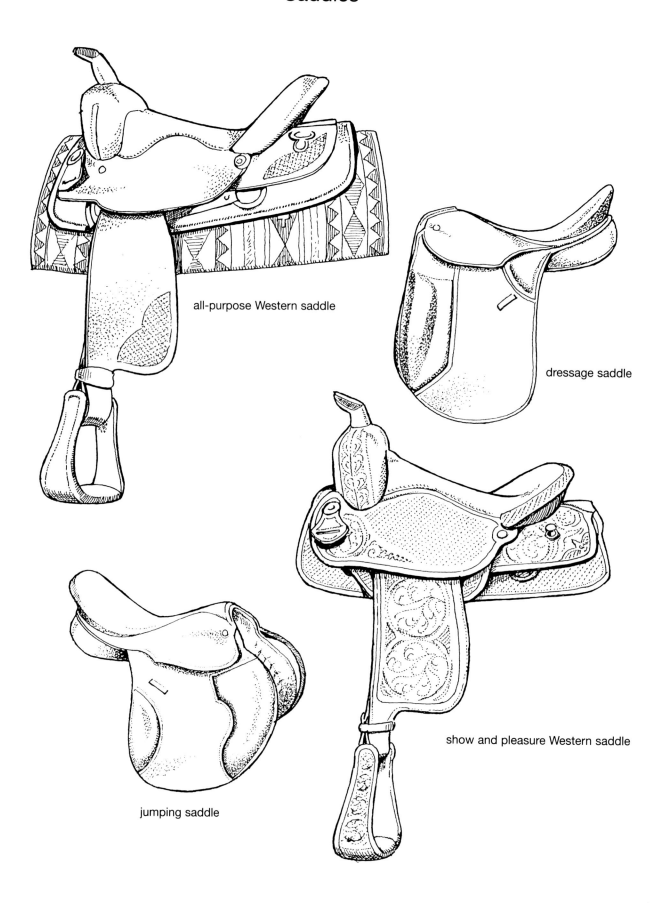

all-purpose Western saddle

dressage saddle

show and pleasure Western saddle

jumping saddle

Saddles

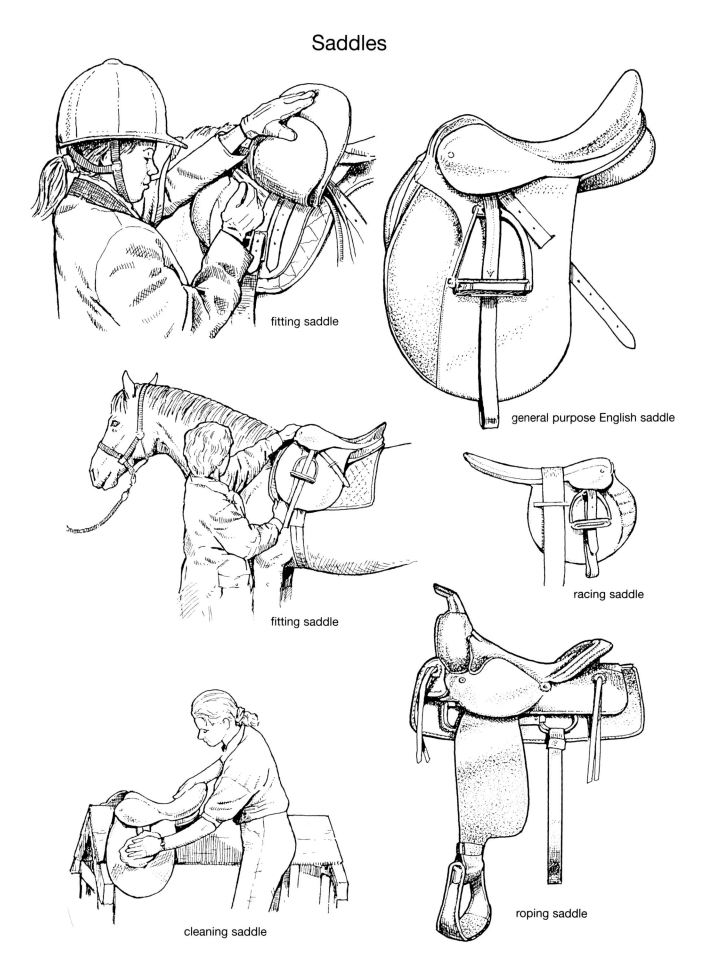

fitting saddle

general purpose English saddle

fitting saddle

racing saddle

cleaning saddle

roping saddle

Stirrups

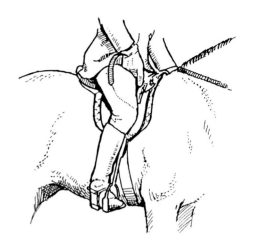

adjusting stirrups

Stirrup Irons and Spurs

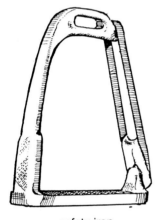

safety iron

modern spur

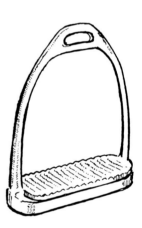

fillis iron with tread

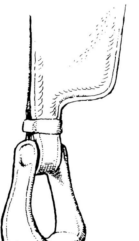

Western stirrup

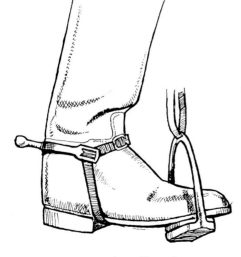

correct position of spur

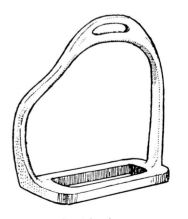

bent leg iron

Bits

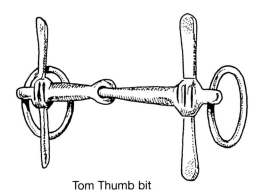

Tom Thumb bit

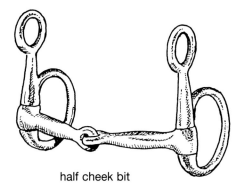

half cheek bit

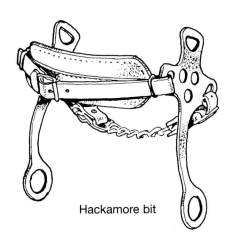

Hackamore bit

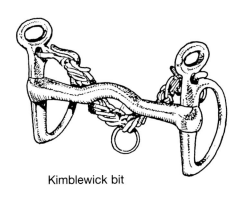

Kimblewick bit

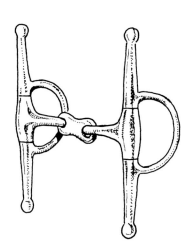

full cheek French link bit

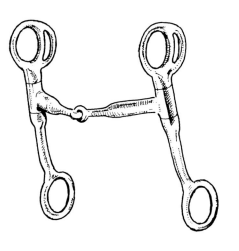

Western Tom Thumb bit (pelham type)

The Bridle

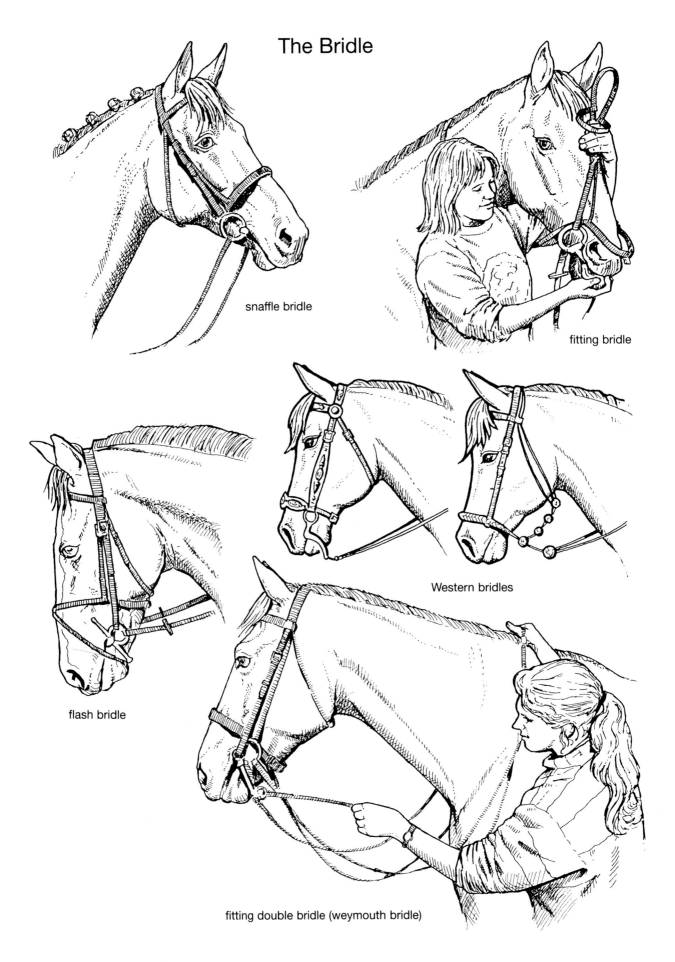

snaffle bridle

fitting bridle

flash bridle

Western bridles

fitting double bridle (weymouth bridle)

The Bridle

measuring bridle

fitting bridle and bit

fitting bit

cleaning tack

fitting bit

cleaning tack

Racing

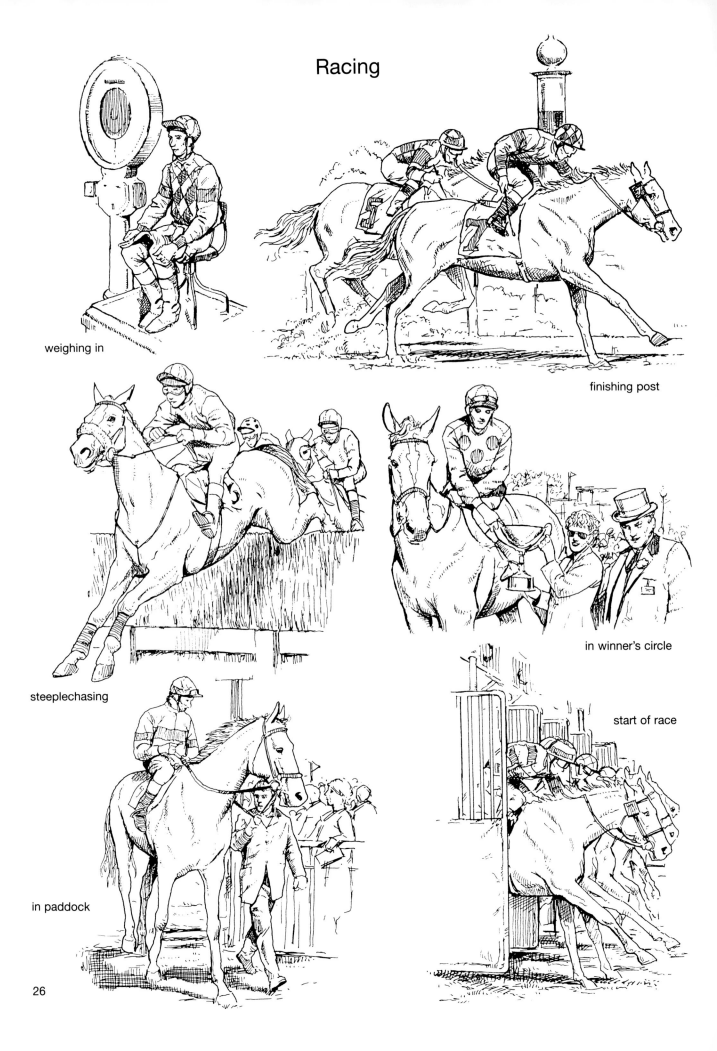

weighing in

finishing post

steeplechasing

in winner's circle

start of race

in paddock

26

Rodeo

prizewinner

showing

bronco riding

barrel racing

steer roping

27

The Horse in Harness

pony and trap

ploughing

horse and cart

trotting

Amish box cart

Schooling or Trained Horses

Western
schooling pacing

dressage

circus horse

Spanish riding school

dressage

Western schooling, Tennessee
walking horse

Show Jumping and Showing

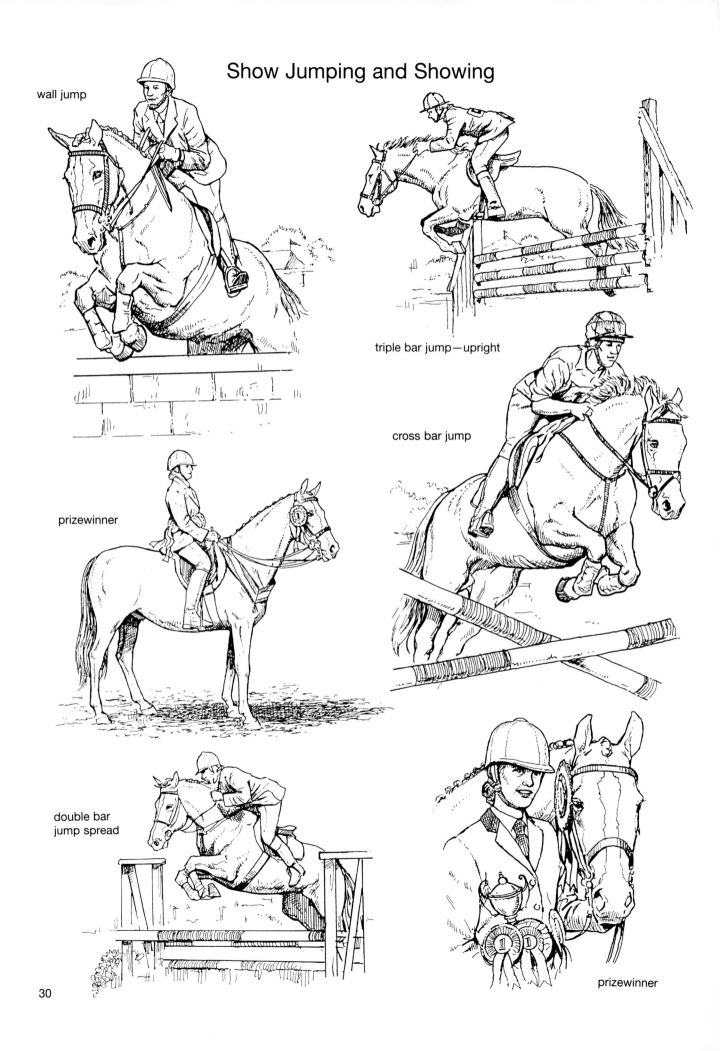

wall jump

triple bar jump—upright

cross bar jump

prizewinner

double bar
jump spread

prizewinner

30

Cross-Country Jumping

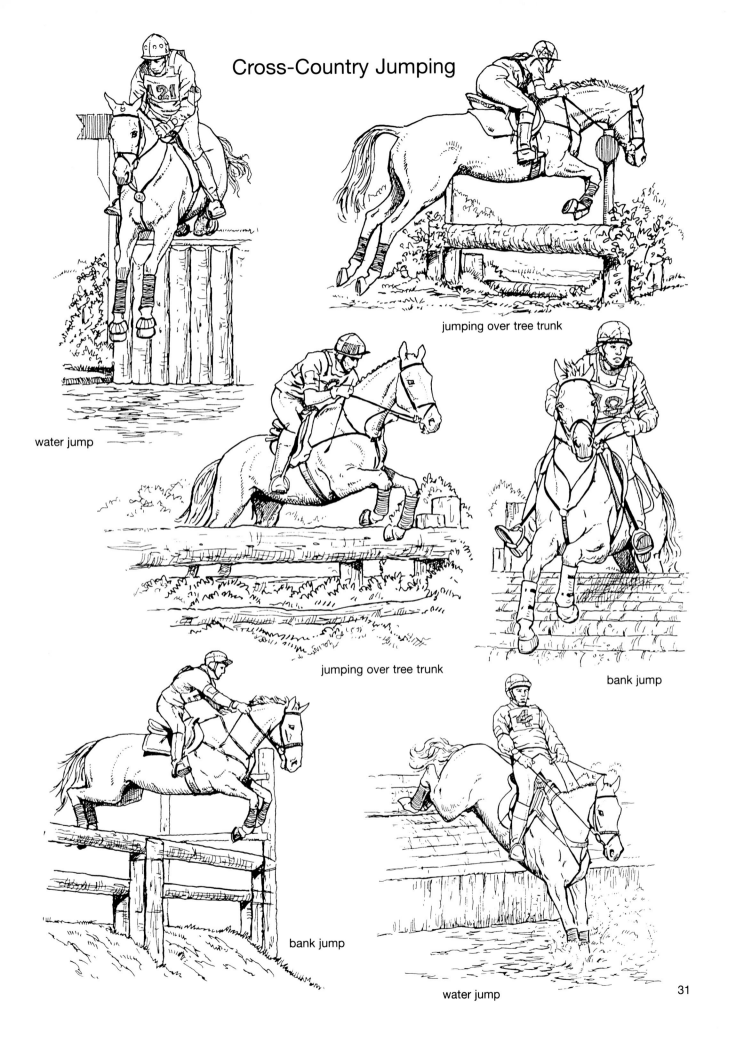

water jump

jumping over tree trunk

jumping over tree trunk

bank jump

bank jump

water jump

31

Polo and Hunting

polo

polo player

foxhunting scenes